Nests and Shelters

WELDON OWEN PTY LTD
Publisher: Sheena Coupe
Senior Designer: Kylie Mulquin
Editorial Coordinators: Sarah Anderson,
Tracey Gibson
Production Manager: Helen Creeke
Production Assistant: Kylie Lawson

Project Editor: Ariana Klepac
Designer: Patricia Ansell
Text: Jan Stradling

05 04 03
10 9 8 7 6 5 4 3

Published in New Zealand by
Shortland Publications,
10 Cawley Street, Ellerslie, Auckland.
Published in the United Kingdom by
Kingscourt/McGraw-Hill,
Shoppenhangers Road, Maidenhead,
Berkshire, SL6 2QL.
Published in Australia by **Mimosa Shortland,**
8 Yarra Street, Hawthorn, Victoria 3122.

Printed in Singapore
ISBN: 0-7699-1261-3

CREDITS AND ACKNOWLEDGMENTS

PICTURE AND ILLUSTRATION CREDITS
[t=top, b=bottom, l=left, r=right, c=centre]
APL 8b. **Dan Cole** 5b. **Corel Corporation** 3b, 7b, 10c. **Simone End** 13bl. **Jon Gittoes** 7t. **Robert Hynes** 14bl.
David Kirshner 13cr. **Frank Knight** 1c, 6b, 12b, 13t. **Rob Mancini** 5tr. **James McKinnon** 11. **PhotoEssentials** banding.
Steve Roberts/Wildlife Art 15. **Barbara Rodanska** 3t, 6t, 9t, 14br. **Peter Schouten** 9b, 16. **Peter Scott** 4b.

Weldon Owen would like to thank the following people for their assistance in the production of this book:
Peta Gorman, Michael Hann, Marney Richardson.

Contents

Nests

Most birds build nests. They build their nests in different places. Some birds build nests in trees. Other birds build nests on the ground.

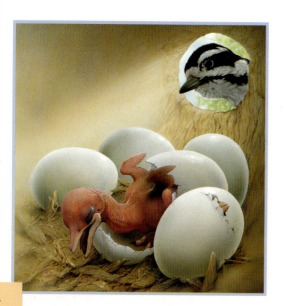

Birds lay their eggs in a nest to keep them safe and warm.

The master weaver bird weaves itself a nest shaped like a basket.

Bower birds *decorate* their nest with colourful things.

Watery Homes

Some animals live in water.
They make shelters
to keep themselves safe
and to raise their young.

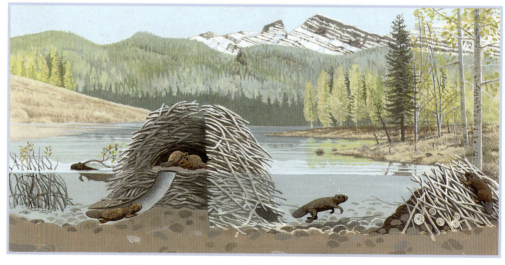

Beavers build a nest called a *lodge*.

Sea otters
sleep in
seaweed
to keep
from drifting.

The beaver builds its lodge from sticks.

Tree-top Homes

Some animals build homes in trees. Some live inside trees, and some live on the branches.

Some squirrels build nests high up in the tree-tops.

Chimpanzees build nests in trees.

Gorillas live on the ground, but sleep in nests in trees at night.

Holes and Burrows

Some animals dig burrows
to live in, where they can keep
safe and raise their babies.
Other animals find holes to live in.

Did You Know?

Prairie dogs dig
burrows that are
joined by tunnels.
An adult always keeps
a lookout for danger.

Prairie dog

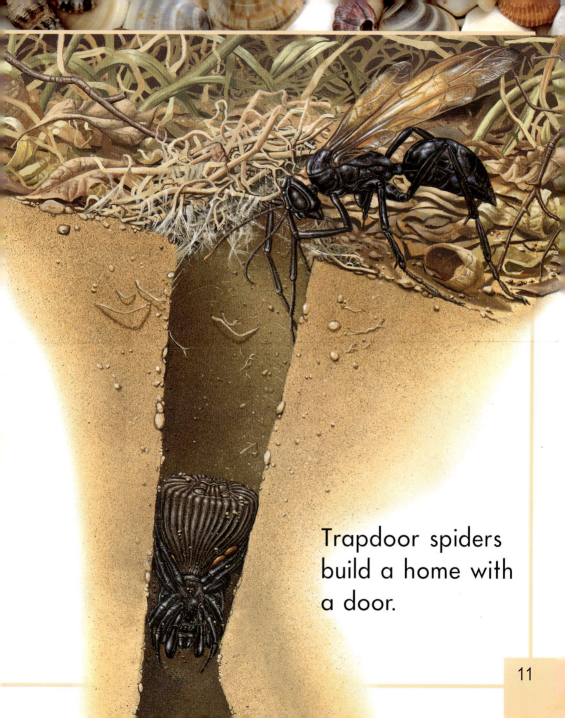

Trapdoor spiders build a home with a door.

Safe from the Weather

Some animals find shelters
for the cold winter months.
These animals sleep a lot.
In very hot places some animals
find shelters from the Sun.

Some bears sleep in holes through winter.

Female polar bears dig *dens*, where they give birth to their young.

A mouse
finds shelter
from the heat
under grass.

Many animals sleep
through winter,
as there is not much
food around.

Insect Nests

Some insects build nests.
They work together to raise their
young and store their food.
Their nests can be very large.

This female wasp
makes a mud pot
to lay her egg in.

Termites build
a huge nest with
many *chambers*.

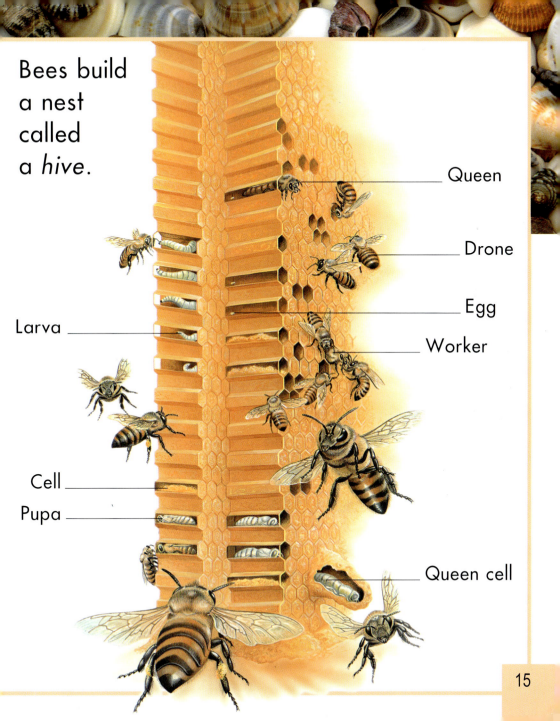

Bees build
a nest
called
a *hive*.

Queen

Drone

Egg

Worker

Larva

Cell

Pupa

Queen cell

15

Glossary

chamber A room

decorate To make something look pretty.

den A hole or shelter where some animals sleep through the cold winter months.

hive A nest built by bees.

lodge A home a beaver builds on a stream, out of sticks and logs.